Saturn

Kate Riggs

CREATIVE EDUCATION
CREATIVE PAPERBACKS

seedlings

Published by Creative Education and Creative Paperbacks
P.O. Box 227, Mankato, Minnesota 56002
Creative Education and Creative Paperbacks
are imprints of The Creative Company
www.thecreativecompany.us

Design by Ellen Huber; production by Joe Kahnke
Art direction by Rita Marshall
Printed in the United States of America

Photographs by Alamy (Aaron Bastin, Tristan3D, Janez Volmajer),
BLACK CAT STUDIOS (Ron Miller), Corbis (13/Ocean), Getty
Images (DEA/G. DAGLI ORTI), NASA (NASA/ESA/JPL/SSI/Cassini
Imaging Team, NASA/JPL, NASA/JPL/Space Science Institute,
NASA/JPL/SSI), Science Source (David A. Hardy, Detlev van
Ravenswaay), Shutterstock (Vadim Sadovski, SirinS), SuperStock
(Science Photo Library, Stocktrek Images)

Library of Congress Cataloging-in-Publication Data
Names: Riggs, Kate, author.
Title: Saturn / Kate Riggs.
Series: Seedlings.
Includes bibliographical references and index.
Summary: A kindergarten-level introduction to the planet
Saturn, covering its orbital process, its moons, and such
defining features as its gases, rings, and name.
Identifiers: ISBN 978-1-60818-918-2 (hardcover) / ISBN 978-1-
62832-534-8 (pbk) / ISBN 978-1-56660-970-8 (eBook)
This title has been submitted for CIP
processing under LCCN 2017938982.

CCSS: RI.K.1, 2, 3, 4, 5, 6, 7;
RI.1.1, 2, 3, 4, 5, 6, 7; RF.K.1, 3; RF.1.1

First Edition HC 9 8 7 6 5 4 3 2 1
First Edition PBK 9 8 7 6 5 4 3 2 1

TABLE OF CONTENTS

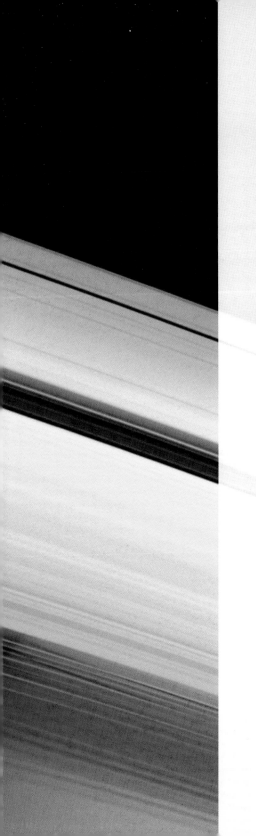

Hello, Saturn!

The ringed planet
Saturn is sixth from
the sun. It is made of
gases. Winds whip
the gases around.

Heat from inside Saturn mixes with the winds. The planet looks like it has bands of yellow and gold.

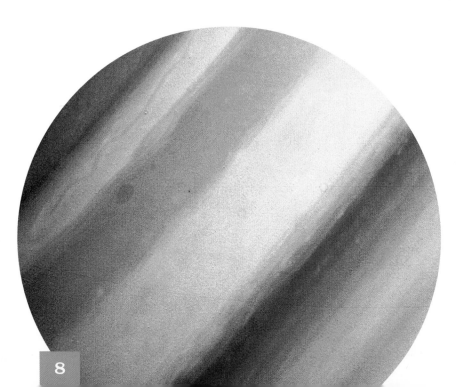

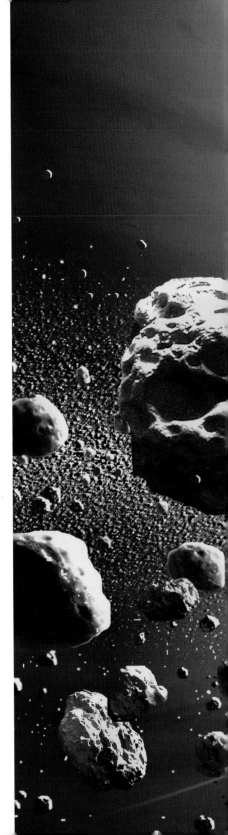

Saturn's rings are made of rock and ice.

Titan is the largest
of Saturn's moons.

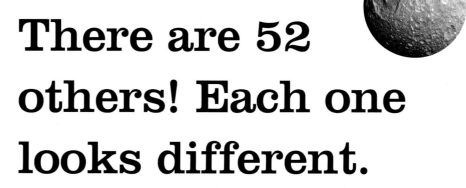

There are 52 others! Each one looks different.

Saturn is the farthest planet we can see from Earth. It takes Saturn 29 years to orbit the sun.

Astronomers study planets. Galileo looked at Saturn in 1610. He used a telescope to see its rings.

Icy chunks of rock circle Saturn. Super-fast winds blow gases.

Goodbye, Saturn!

cloud bands

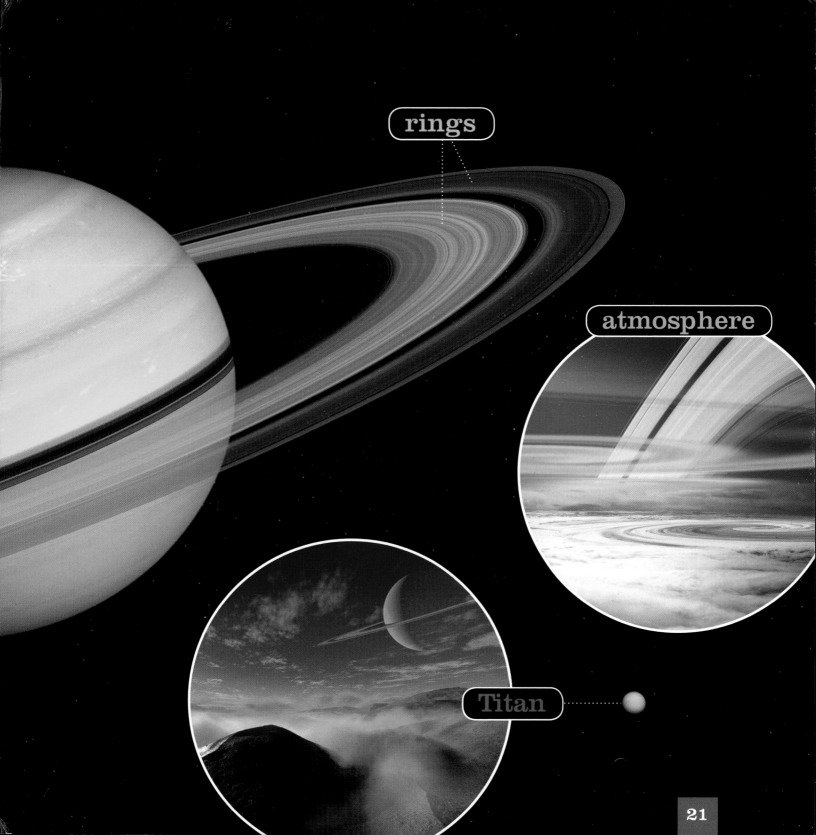

rings

atmosphere

Titan

Words to Know

orbit: the path a planet, moon, or other object takes around something else in outer space

planet: a rounded object that moves around a star

telescope: a viewing tool that makes objects that are far away appear closer

Read More

Heos, Bridget. *Do You Really Want to Visit Saturn?* Mankato, Minn.: Amicus, 2014.

Loewen, Nancy. *Ringed Giant: The Planet Saturn.* Minneapolis: Picture Window Books, 2008.

Websites

NASA Jet Propulsion Laboratory: Kids
http://www.jpl.nasa.gov/kids/
Build a spacecraft or play a planetary game.

National Geographic Kids: Pluto's Secret
http://kids.nationalgeographic.com/games/adventure/plutos-secret/
Find out more about our solar system!

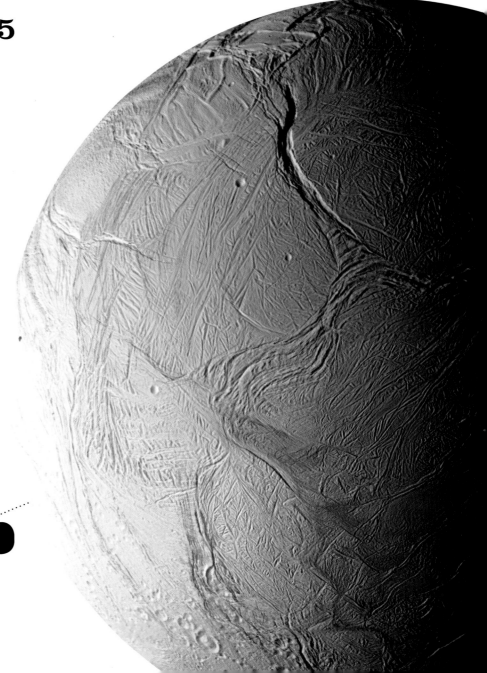

Index

Enceladus